A Guide to College Survival

WILLIAM F. BROWN
WAYNE H. HOLTZMAN

Illustrations by Will Thomson

The American College Testing Program
Iowa City, Iowa

Library of Congress Cataloging-in-Publication Data

Brown, William Frank, 1920-
A guide to college survival.

Includes bibliographical references and index.
1. Study, Method of—Handbooks, manuals, etc.
2. College students—United States—Time management—Handbooks, manuals, etc. I. Holtzman, Wayne H.
II. Title.
LB2395.B76 1987 378'.1702812 86-28765
ISBN 0-937734-12-8 (pbk.)

Previous edition © 1972, 1983 by Effective Study Materials, San Marcos, Texas (ISBN 0-13-369306-6).

Contents

Preface

The many observations and recommendations in *A Guide to College Survival* are derived from working with students for 35 years. One recommendation is especially appropriate to single out for attention in this preface: "If you are to survive as an entering freshman, you must realize that the first year in college is *not* grade 13 of high school."

Unfortunately, far too many college freshmen fail to realize this difference in time, or at least fail to change their attitudes and behaviors accordingly. For these students—many of whom would be considered, by any customary standard, above average in ability—the personal, social, and academic adjustments required by the first year of college prove to be too great. And year after year, despite the efforts of high schools to turn out better prepared graduates, more than 30 percent of all college freshmen fail to become sophomores. Others survive (though barely), and even go on to graduate, but get considerably less out of college than they could.

It does not have to be that way—not if students know what to expect of the freshman year and how to adjust to the challenges they will encounter. The original edition of *A Guide to College Survival* was written to give students practical, timely information of proven value in getting better college grades. For this same reason, ACT is now making this revised edition available nationally.

This book offers a solid core of information about improving study organization, study techniques, and study motivation. *A Guide to College Survival* also emphasizes that an equally important key to success is the student's maturity and willingness to accept personal responsibility for his or her decisions and actions. The great increase in the amount and complexity of academic work is only one part of the adjustment that the newly admitted freshman faces on campus. The other part involves both learning to cope with the diversity of social activities that vie with academic courses for a share of the student's limited time—and learning to discipline oneself in the absence of the social restraints and school-related reminders formerly provided by parents and teachers. The freshman who cannot handle the freedom of the college campus, who cannot put studies before social activities, generally loses that freedom after one or two grading periods.

As a college freshman or a college-bound high school junior or senior (or the parent, spouse, or friend of such a student), you may be interested in knowing that *A Guide to College Survival* is more than just another how-to-study textbook. It is a complete, practical guide for adjusting personally, socially, and academically to the demands of college life. The adjustment problems that we identify and the strategies that we recommend are based both on research and on the suggestions of students who succeeded in making the most of their college education. Whether this book is used for a college orientation program, in a study skills course, or as a self-help handbook, it can make a significant difference for students of all levels of ability.

In a very real sense, this revised edition of *A Guide to College Survival* is dedicated to new and prospective college freshmen. We sincerely hope that you will find it helpful in ensuring your survival in college.

William F. Brown
Wayne H. Holtzman

1

Surviving (and Succeeding!) in College

Did you know . . .

. . . that only six or seven out of ten beginning freshmen survive beyond the first year of college and that only four or five of the ten succeed in earning a bachelor's degree in four years?

. . . that many high-ability freshmen are underachievers, never realizing their academic potential and in some cases failing while others of low to average ability progress steadily through college and even graduate with honors?

. . . that deficient study skills and negative or indifferent scholastic motivation are two major causes of difficulty in college?

. . . that study habits and academic attitudes can be improved through systematic relearning?

Factors in College Survival and Success

College faculty members, academic advisers, and personal counselors are constantly confronted with students who receive poor grades despite apparently superior intelligence. There are also students of ordinary scholastic aptitude who earn excellent scholarship records. Educators have long been challenged to explain why many students achieve far below or far above their measured academic ability.

The results of research into this issue suggest that your measured scholastic aptitude or ability reveals only your current potential for educational attainment. In addition to your academic ability, other factors such as previous academic achievement, adjustment to academic life, and attitude toward academic work affect your performance in college.

Academic Ability

Your intellectual capacity for learning the material presented in your courses is known as your *academic ability,* or learning potential. People differ greatly in their mental capacity for this kind of learning. In fact, two individuals who have identical total scores on an intelligence test will often show great variance when they are compared on specific aptitudes being evaluated. It is, therefore, very important that you know your potential strengths and weaknesses for different kinds of academic learning and that you plan your educational program accordingly.

Academic Achievement

"Before I take history, maybe I'd better take remedial reading!"

Your *academic achievement,* or learning background, is the foundation of knowledge that you have already acquired. While an "uneven" foundation may be a consequence of disadvantaged opportunity or inadequate instruction, it may also be due to insufficient study or failure to learn how to learn. For the beginning freshman, effective reading and writing skills are two of the most essential requirements for success in nearly all college courses. Because reading and writing are so important, you should make every effort to correct quickly any deficiencies in your reading speed and comprehension or in your writing mechanics and effectiveness.

Academic Adjustment

The term *academic adjustment* refers to your mastery of basic study skills and your efficiency in performing academic activities. Many beginning freshmen, for example, must change their learning behavior in order to cope with such unfamiliar procedures as formal lectures in large auditoriums and all-important final examinations. Also, your efficiency in doing your academic assignments will depend in part on your use of effective techniques for organizing and accomplishing your study activities.

Academic Attitude

Your feelings and expectations about college as well as your desire for academic learning compose your *academic attitude.* Pressures stemming from your interaction with family and peer group members can affect your scholastic success through their impact upon your academic values and aspirations. Thus, your educational beliefs can be positive or negative and your educational objectives can be long-term or short-range. If your motivation is indifferent and your academic goals are vague, you will probably have difficulty when the assignments pile up. Knowing what you want from college and why you want it is the key to having a good academic attitude.

These four personal factors are among the keys to your scholastic success and satisfaction. Another student may be brighter than you or may have had the benefit of better instruction than you received in high school. These are two factors over which you have little control. But given a *reasonably* good background, you can do as well as or better than that student if you are interested in your courses, if you want to earn good grades, and if you try to adapt yourself to the college environment and its academic demands. Your academic attitude is a crucial factor in determining whether or not you will put forth the necessary effort.

Increasing Your Chances for Survival and Success

You can increase your chances for academic survival and success even if you find yourself deficient in one, two, three, or all four of the factors just discussed. There are two main ways of doing this—compensating for deficiencies with extra time and effort, and correcting deficiencies by developing better study habits.

Extra Time and Effort

Suppose that you find your academic background or ability to be below average for learning the material presented in one of your courses. Your solution must be to compensate for your disadvantage by putting extra time and effort into your studying. In comparison with the other students, you may take twice as long to prepare your assignments, but you will find that you can learn the material if you make the added effort. On the other hand, your difficulty may stem largely from deficient reading, writing, or study skills. Here, your solution should be to undertake a systematic program designed to correct the deficiency as quickly as possible. You can improve your reading comprehension, for example, provided you are willing to do the extra work and exercise the self-discipline required to overcome your poor reading skills.

"Let's see, 3,940 pages of reading at 10 pages an hour—that will take a lot of compensating!"

If you refuse to put forth the necessary time and effort, however, nothing is going to help you become a successful student. You must have the desire to learn if you are to master the material presented in textbooks and lectures. Desire to learn doesn't mean that you necessarily enjoy studying.

"Well, it was either go to work or go to college, so . . . ."

Desire to learn means that you sincerely want to know more about yourself and about the world you live in. It also means that you want to master the required knowledge and skills for entering a specific occupational area. Without the desire to learn, you are seriously handicapped at the outset.

Of great importance, too, is the need to develop a keen interest in the subject matter of your courses. Without this, you will have little incentive to become skillful in the art of studying. Ask yourself why you are going to college. Is it because your friends are going to college or because your parents believe that it is the best thing to do? Is it because you have heard that college life, social activities, sports, and campus politics are lots of fun? Is it because going to college is a good way to put off going to work at a full-time job? Maybe you have heard that "everyone" goes on to college and have concluded that you'll have to go too. While all of these are important considerations, you will probably find college difficult unless you have a genuine desire to prepare yourself for a future career, to learn something about yourself and the world you live in, or to acquire knowledge for its own sake.

Better Study Habits

Part of the challenge of adjusting to college is the development of systematic and efficient study habits. While exceptionally bright students might get satisfactory grades without organizing their study habits properly, the chances are they could do much better by rethinking the way they approach the task of learning academic materials. Similarly, some failing students could make passing grades by careful planning and organization of study habits, and could probably do so without increasing their study time.

Developing study habits and skills is similar to becoming skillful in any other activity. Just as learning to swim or play basketball takes considerable practice, requires an interest in learning the skill, and sometimes calls for the help of a coach, acquiring efficient study methods takes patient practice and sometimes outside help from a counselor or teacher. In addition to these sources of help, there are several excellent books dealing with the art of studying. Your school or college librarian can help you locate appropriate references for further reading on the topic.

A college freshman quickly discovers that there are two facets of college life—the academic and the social. You should realize that excessive involvement in either one can prove to be unwise. To succeed fully in college, you should participate actively in at least some of the diverse social activities of college life as well as in the formal academic programs. The important thing, of course, is to be realistic and always remember that your academic requirements should receive first priority.

You will also discover that both facets of college life require adjustments on your part—adjustments to the demands of academic work, and adjustments to social life outside the classroom. The extent of your adjustments will depend, in part, on whether you reside on campus in an apartment or dormitory with other students, or commute to campus from your home. In either case, the way in which you adjust socially will probably have a direct influence on the effectiveness of your academic adjustment.

Living on Campus

For the on-campus resident, most personal and social adjustments can be grouped into four areas:

1. Development of self-reliance and independence
2. Development of effective relations with one or more roommates
3. Coping effectively with the problems of group living
4. Participation in extracurricular activities

As a dormitory resident, you will find that you are responsible for your own clothing care and most or all of your housekeeping. You may also find that you and your roommate or roommates have very different attitudes—about studying, politics, money, religion, drinking, sex, and many other things. You will discover that, if you are to succeed in adjusting to group living, dormitory rules and regulations must be accepted along with the disturbances and distractions that come with the loss of individual privacy. Finally, you will realize that the number and variety of extracurricular activities available to you can distract you from your studies if allowed to.

"My roomie? Oh, he's okay, but he takes his studying too seriously."

The following suggestions will help you adjust to on-campus living.

1. Treat your roommate as an equal. Don't give orders, make unreasonable demands, or expect favors.

2. Respect your roommate's right to privacy. Don't pry into his or her private affairs or expect to share his or her activities unless invited.

3. Keep borrowing to an absolute minimum. Don't expect your roommate to loan money, clothing, jewelry, etc.

4. Avoid trying to "reform" or "correct" your roommate. Don't expect your roommate to conform to your standards or take up your beliefs.

5. Work out a mutually acceptable division of chores. Don't wait for your roommate to take care of the housekeeping.

6. Make a sincere effort to be friendly to everyone. Don't withdraw into a shell or forget common courtesy.

7. Accept routine inconveniences without complaint. Don't gripe continuously about little annoyances that are really insignificant.

8. Keep your promises and commitments without exception. Don't break appointments or renege on agreements.

9. Respect the efforts of others to study. Don't cause interruptions or make unnecessary noises.

10. Limit your participation in extracurricular activities. Don't join everything in sight just for prestige.

11. Participate fully in one or two carefully selected extracurricular activities. Don't shirk the responsibilities and obligations of membership once you have joined a group.

12. Prepare and live within a realistic budget. Try not to ask your parents for extra money too often.

13. Learn to say "no" when social activities interfere with academic requirements. Don't let undone assignments pile up due to poor time management.

Living off Campus

For the student living off campus, most personal and social adjustments can be grouped into two areas:

1. Achieving campus identification as a fully involved student
2. Coping with the continuing demands of life within your family

If you are living at home, you may find that you are spending considerable time commuting between home and campus. You may also discover that your use of college facilities and your participation in extracurricular activities are limited by the amount of time that you are on campus. Carpooling arrangements or part-time employment may further complicate the situation.

The off-campus student sometimes feels a lack of identification with college life. Instead of making friends and attending social activities on campus, you are likely to limit your friendships and social life to the off-campus community. Furthermore, your involvement in family activities and your concern about family matters will probably remain undiminished while you are living at home.

"What happens around here after classes? Sorry, I don't know—I commute."

The following suggestions will help you adjust to being a commuting student.

1. Spread your classes out. Don't bunch classes together on a few days in order to reduce your time on campus.
2. Make new friends on campus at every opportunity. Don't hesitate to take the initiative.
3. Join and participate fully in at least one extracurricular activity. Don't avoid becoming involved.
4. Use the library as much as possible. Don't do all your assignments off campus unless you absolutely must.
5. Discuss your situation with your family. Don't let excessive family commitments cause you to get poor grades.

Getting Along With Your Professors

Whether you live on or off campus, you will soon find that teacher-student relations in college are very different from those you experienced in high school. Your college professors and instructors will be more demanding of your best efforts and less tolerant of your best excuses. They will expect you to behave like a fully responsible adult. Consequently, some of your professors may seem aloof and unsympathetic when you first try to communicate with them. Most of them, however, are genuinely interested in you as a student.

You will encounter both good and poor professors, just as they will have both superior and inferior students. Such variation is inevitable in any large-scale human enterprise. The real challenge is for students and professors to work together toward common goals.

The following suggestions will help you achieve positive working relationships with your professors and with the instructors, lecturers, and teaching assistants you'll be more likely to encounter during your freshman year.

"Then when I asked my professor what I should do to pull up my grades, she suggested that studying *might help!"*

1. Be in your seat ready to begin work when the class starts. Don't expect a delayed entrance to make a favorable impression on anybody.
2. Be alert and attentive to all class activities. Don't alienate your professor by falling asleep or daydreaming in class.
3. Learn your professor's likes and dislikes concerning class discussion. Don't waste class time with idle questions or quibbling over minor points.
4. Prepare your written assignments as neatly and accurately as possible. Don't let messy or careless work create the impression that you don't care.
5. Accept and learn from any oral or written corrections offered by your professors. Don't take such criticisms personally.
6. Form your own opinion about each of your professors. Don't allow the opinions of other students to prejudice your own judgment.
7. Work extra hard to compensate if you find that you dislike one of your professors. Don't complain, act aloof, or show hostility.
8. Avoid excuses and flattery when asking your professors for help. Don't expect your professors to devote extra time to you unless you are straightforward with them.
9. Accept responsibility for your mistakes. Don't blame your professors.

The Decision Is Yours

Will your college career end in success or failure? You, and you alone, have the power to decide. You will get out of college exactly what you put into it. In this respect, college living is like all of life itself.

Using the Study Skills Checklists

Your ability to learn and your educational background are not the primary concerns of this book. This book is primarily concerned with factors over which you have direct and immediate control—your study skills and your motivation to learn.

Your success in academic work involves two processes—organizing your time and effort for effective learning, and employing proven techniques of effective study. These two processes, together with your motivation to learn, provide a basis for assessing and improving your study skills. Regardless of your academic ability or background, you can benefit by examining the adequacy of your present study organization, study techniques, and study motivation.

About the Checklists

The Study Skills Checklists are three short surveys that you can use to assess your strengths and weaknesses in study organization, techniques, and motivation. Each checklist consists of 20 questions to be answered "Yes" or "No." Although the Study Skills Checklists will help you identify any study problems that are reducing your effectiveness in academic work, the checklists do not measure the scope or the intensity of study problems. Because your answers may be affected by your awareness of your problems and your willingness to reveal them, think of your scores as *estimates* of your self-reported strengths and weaknesses.

Questions on the Study Organization Checklist are divided equally between two skill areas. Questions 1-10 deal with common problems connected with effective use of study time; questions 11-20 deal with common problems associated with efficient organization of study environment.

The 20-question Study Techniques Checklist includes four questions for each of five different skill areas. Questions 1-4, 5-8, 9-12, 13-16, and 17-20 deal with the most common problems associated with reading textbooks, taking class notes, writing reports, preparing for tests, and taking tests, respectively.

Questions 1-14 on the Study Motivation Checklist deal with common problems arising from an indifferent or negative attitude about the value of education. Problems stemming from negativism or indifference toward teachers are covered by questions 15-20.

Completing the Checklists

You can complete all three checklists, on your own, in about 15 minutes. First, remove the answer sheet (on the next page) from this book. Then read the checklists and answer each of the 60 questions "Yes" or "No." Record your answers on the answer sheet.

There are no "right" or "wrong" answers to these checklists. The *best* answers are those that accurately reflect what you do when you study and how you feel about your education. Be honest with yourself. Answer each question according to what you are in the habit of doing and feeling, not according to what you think you *should* do or feel, or according to what you think *others* might do or feel.

Work as quickly as you can without being careless, and do not spend too much time on any one question. To get the most useful results, answer all of the questions.

STUDY SKILLS CHECKLISTS

ANSWER SHEET

Directions: Answer each question "Yes" or "No" and check the appropriate box.

STUDY ORGANIZATION CHECKLIST

	Yes	No
1.	☐	☐
2.	☐	☐
3.	☐	☐
4.	☐	☐
5.	☐	☐
6.	☐	☐
7.	☐	☐
8.	☐	☐
9.	☐	☐
10.	☐	☐
11.	☐	☐
12.	☐	☐
13.	☐	☐
14.	☐	☐
15.	☐	☐
16.	☐	☐
17.	☐	☐
18.	☐	☐
19.	☐	☐
20.	☐	☐

Score ________

STUDY TECHNIQUES CHECKLIST

	Yes	No
1.	☐	☐
2.	☐	☐
3.	☐	☐
4.	☐	☐
5.	☐	☐
6.	☐	☐
7.	☐	☐
8.	☐	☐
9.	☐	☐
10.	☐	☐
11.	☐	☐
12.	☐	☐
13.	☐	☐
14.	☐	☐
15.	☐	☐
16.	☐	☐
17.	☐	☐
18.	☐	☐
19.	☐	☐
20.	☐	☐

Score ________

STUDY MOTIVATION CHECKLIST

	Yes	No
1.	☐	☐
2.	☐	☐
3.	☐	☐
4.	☐	☐
5.	☐	☐
6.	☐	☐
7.	☐	☐
8.	☐	☐
9.	☐	☐
10.	☐	☐
11.	☐	☐
12.	☐	☐
13.	☐	☐
14.	☐	☐
15.	☐	☐
16.	☐	☐
17.	☐	☐
18.	☐	☐
19.	☐	☐
20.	☐	☐

Score ________

TOTAL SCORE ☐

1. Do you usually put off preparing themes and reports until the last minute?
2. Do you frequently find that you are too tired or sleepy to study efficiently?
3. Do you often fail to complete out-of-class assignments on time?
4. Do you frequently spend time reading magazines, watching television, or exchanging gossip when you should be studying?
5. Do social or athletic activities frequently cause you to neglect your academic assignments?
6. Do you usually wait a day or more before reviewing the notes taken in class?
7. Do you usually spend any free time between 8 a.m. and 4 p.m. in activities other than studying?
8. Do you sometimes suddenly discover that an assignment is due sooner than you thought it was?
9. Do you often get behind in one course because of having to study for another?
10. Do you seem to accomplish very little in relation to the amount of time that you spend studying?
11. Is your study desk directly facing a window, door, or other source of distraction?
12. Do you usually keep photographs or other mementos on your study desk?
13. Do you frequently study while lying in bed or lounging in a comfortable chair?
14. Does the light from your lamp create a glare where you study?
15. Is your study desk often so cluttered that you don't have enough room to study efficiently?
16. Do visitors to your room often interrupt your studying?
17. Do you often study with a television, radio, or stereo playing?
18. Are magazines, posters, or hobby materials visible from where you usually study?
19. Is your studying often disturbed by activities and noises from outside your room?
20. Is your studying often slowed down because needed books or study materials are not on hand?

Study Techniques Checklist

1. Do you normally begin reading a textbook assignment without first surveying the unit headings and illustrative materials?
2. Do you frequently skip over the figures, graphs, and tables in a reading assignment?
3. Do you frequently have difficulty picking out the important points in a reading assignment?
4. Do you frequently catch yourself thinking about something totally unrelated to what you are reading?
5. Do you frequently have difficulty understanding your class notes when you try to read them later?
6. Do you frequently get behind in your notetaking because you can't write fast enough?
7. Are your class notes usually a disorganized mess shortly after a semester begins?
8. Do you normally try to record your instructor's exact words when taking class notes?
9. Do you normally copy material word for word when taking reading notes?
10. Do you often have difficulty selecting an appropriate topic for a term paper or report?
11. Do you frequently have trouble organizing the content of a term paper or report?
12. Do you usually prepare the outline after the term paper or report is written?
13. Do you sometimes prepare for a test by memorizing formulas, definitions, or rules that you do not clearly understand?
14. Do you generally have difficulty deciding what and how to study for multiple-choice tests?
15. Do you normally have difficulty organizing the material to be learned into logical study units?
16. Do you depend mainly on last-minute cramming in preparing for tests?
17. Do you frequently turn in your test paper without carefully checking for careless errors?
18. Are you frequently unable to finish answering essay questions within the allotted time?
19. Do you frequently lose points on true-false tests because you failed to read the questions carefully?
20. Do you often spend too much time on the first half of a test and thus have to rush through the last half?

1. Do you often lose interest in your studies after the first few days or weeks of class?
2. Do you generally believe in doing only enough to get a passing grade in your courses?
3. Do you frequently feel confused and undecided as to what your educational and vocational goals should be?
4. Do you often feel that getting an education is not worth the time and effort it requires of you?
5. Do you believe that having a good time and getting your full share of fun out of life is more important than studying?
6. Do you often spend the class period doodling or daydreaming instead of listening to the instructor?
7. Are you frequently unable to concentrate on your studies because of restlessness, moodiness, boredom, etc.?
8. Do you often feel that you are taking courses that are of little practical value to you?
9. Do you often feel like dropping out of school and getting a job?
10. Do you often feel that your courses are not preparing you to meet adult problems?
11. Is your studying often a hit-or-miss proposition depending on the mood you are in?
12. Do you often dread reading textbooks because you feel that they are dull and boring?
13. Do you normally wait until a test is scheduled before reading textbook assignments or reviewing lecture notes?
14. Do you usually think of examinations as ordeals that can't be escaped and must somehow be survived?
15. Do you often feel that your instructors don't understand the needs and interests of students?
16. Do you often feel that your instructors require too much studying outside of class?
17. Do you normally hesitate to ask your instructors for help with difficult assignments?
18. Do you frequently feel that your instructors are out of touch with present-day issues and events?
19. Do you generally feel reluctant to discuss your educational or vocational plans with your instructors?
20. Do you often speak critically about your instructors to other students?

Using Your Checklist Results

For each of the three checklists, figure your score by counting the number of questions that you answered "No." Record each total at the bottom of the appropriate column on the answer sheet. Compute your total score by adding the separate scores for the three checklists. Record your total score in the box at the lower right-hand corner of the answer sheet.

To interpret your scores, you might use Table 2.1, Study Skills Checklists Comparison Table for College Freshmen (page 23), and the Diagnostic Profile that follows it. The Comparison Table and Diagnostic Profile are based on the scores of a norm group—or comparison sample—of 3,426 beginning college freshmen tested at Southwest Texas State University, Saint Augustine's College, and Lamar University during 1977-83. By referring to the Comparison Table and Diagnostic Profile, you can evaluate your scores in terms of the five broad interpretive categories provided. For example, a score of 14 on the Study Organization Checklist could be viewed as "Above Average" on the basis of interpretive categories given in the table.

Use the following three-step procedure in interpreting your scores. First, find and circle each of your scores in the appropriate score column of the Comparison Table. Second, determine the interpretive category for each of your scores. Third, transfer your scores and interpretive categories to the appropriate blanks on the Diagnostic Profile (page 24), then read the section "What Your Scores Mean."

When you've completed the Diagnostic Profile, review your results carefully, giving particular attention to any score that rated as "Below Average" or "Low." To take action on any study skills problems suggested by such a score, begin by turning back to the appropriate checklist and rereading each question that you answered "Yes." As you do so, ask yourself:

1. How serious is the problem?
2. What is causing the problem?
3. What can I do to correct the problem?

Then read the chapter(s) of this book covering any study skills area(s)—organization, techniques, or motivation—for which you scored "Below Average" or "Low." Even if you scored "Average," "Above Average," or "High" on the checklists, you will find it helpful to read these chapters. They provide practical suggestions for developing more efficient study organization, more effective study techniques, and more positive study motivation.

TABLE 2.1

Study Skills Checklists Comparison Table for College Freshmen

Study Organization Score	Study Techniques Score	Study Motivation Score	Total Score	Interpretive Category
16-20	17-20	18-20	50-60	High
13-15	14-16	15-17	40-49	Above Average
12	13	14	37-39	Average
9-11	9-12	11-13	27-36	Below Average
0-8	0-8	0-10	0-26	Low

Note. Data are based on the scores of 3,426 beginning college freshmen tested at Southwest Texas State University, San Marcos, Texas, in 1977; at Saint Augustine's College, Raleigh, North Carolina, in 1982; and at Lamar University, Beaumont, Texas, in 1983.

Diagnostic Profile

Making a Profile of Your Scores

To make your Diagnostic Profile, read the four statements below and fill in the blanks with your scores on the Study Skills Checklists and the corresponding interpretive categories from the Comparison Table. Then read the section about the meaning and limitations of your scores.

• **Study Organization Score:** This provides an estimate of my lack of problems in using my study time and organizing my study environment. When compared to the scores of a sample of beginning college freshmen, my score of ____ could be interpreted as ________________________.

• **Study Techniques Score:** This provides an estimate of my lack of problems in reading textbooks, taking class notes, writing reports, preparing for tests, and taking tests. When compared to the scores of a sample of beginning college freshmen, my score of ____ could be interpreted as ________________________.

• **Study Motivation Score:** This provides an estimate of my lack of problems in accepting educational practices and procedures and adjusting to academic activities and requirements. When compared to the scores of a sample of beginning college freshmen, my score of ____ could be interpreted as ________________________.

• **Total Score:** This combines my scores on all three checklists to provide an overall estimate of my lack of problems in study behavior and motivation. When compared to the scores of a sample of beginning college freshmen, my score of ____ could be interpreted as ________________________.

What Your Scores Mean

As you interpret your scores on the Study Skills Checklists, keep the following cautions in mind:

1. If you used the Comparison Table, your interpretive categories can be meaningful only to the extent that you resemble the students in the norm group in terms of your characteristics, situation, and response tendencies.

2. People differ in their responsiveness to self-report checklists. Some will acknowledge all problems, however minor; others will acknowledge only problems they consider major.

3. You may have misread or misunderstood one or more of the checklist questions.

4. You may not have acknowledged or marked one or more serious study problems.

5. A "Yes"/"No" response format cannot show the intensity or seriousness of a problem.

6. Any score is just one estimate of your true ability and should be interpreted in that light. If you answered questions a second time, it is unlikely that you would get exactly the same score.

Because of the limitations of the checklist process, low scores on the Study Skills Checklists shouldn't be viewed with alarm. Instead, regard any low score as only a warning—a means of calling your attention to an area where your present study skills probably need to be strengthened. Similarly, a high score doesn't necessarily mean that you couldn't benefit by improving your study skills in that area.

High scores on the checklists tend to be characteristic of students who make good grades and find their academic work challenging and interesting; low scores tend to be characteristic of students who make poor grades and find their academic work difficult or uninteresting. For this reason, your scores on the Study Skills Checklists not only can indicate any problems you may have in the areas measured but also may help you anticipate the level of future academic achievement you might attain if identified problems go uncorrected.

Efficient study habits and positive study attitudes are important factors in scholastic success. Improving your study skills is up to you; the remaining chapters of this book can help.

3

Organizing for Effective Study

Research has consistently demonstrated that efficient management of time is an important factor in scholastic success. Time is easy to waste and impossible to regain. At college, opportunities for social activities will continually surround you. If you let social activities take precedence over your studies, you will sooner or later discover that the little time left in the school term cannot possibly stretch to cover all of the studying that you have put off.

Most college freshmen report that the time required to prepare their out-of-class assignments is double or triple what it was in high school. Yet most beginning college students waste a surprising amount of time in aimless, unproductive activity. For example, how would *you* spend a one-hour "free" period between two morning classes? If you spend the time talking with friends, walking around the campus, or dropping by the snack bar instead of studying in the library, you are misusing perhaps the most valuable study hour in your entire day. An example of this kind of time-wasting is shown in Figure 3.1.

Or, what about your evening study periods? Quite often you may say to yourself: "Tonight right after supper I am going to shut myself up in my room to study for three hours without disturbance." While this is a fine objective, more likely than not you begin talking about something interesting at the dinner table, you receive a phone call from a friend, you decide to watch a television program for "just a few minutes," or you let someone talk you into going to a movie or basketball game, thinking that you'll have plenty of time when you get back to read that history assignment. Thus, the time that you had set aside for study has been spent on other activities and you will probably be unprepared when exams roll around.

"Look, we can study any old time, but this movie tonight is can't-miss."

An Hour Well Spent?

Here is how one college freshman spent the hour between two morning classes.

TIME	ACTIVITY
8:51	Leaves history class, talks briefly with friends outside.
8:54	Starts for library.
8:56	Meets friend, discusses plans for weekend football game.
8:59	Finishes discussion, heads for library.
9:02	Arrives at library, stops friend to check on when English theme is due.
9:04	Finishes discussion, enters library.
9:08	Settles down, starts to read history assignment.
9:14	Realizes history assignment is not due till next week, decides to work on tomorrow's English assignment instead.
9:15	Spots friend at another table, decides to check on English assignment.
9:16	Checks English assignment, discusses football team's prospects in game.
9:20	Finishes conversation, returns to study.
9:21	Counts number of pages in English assignment, realizes assignment cannot be completed in thirty minutes, debates future course of action.
9:23	Decides to read as much as possible anyway.
9:27	Finds English assignment boring, decides to check over math homework instead.
9:31	Discovers math homework has not been completed, begins working remaining problems.
9:40	Completes second math problem, recognizes impossibility of working remaining ten problems in fifteen minutes, debates future course of action.
9:42	Decides to adjourn to coffee shop.
9:45	Arrives at coffee shop, purchases coffee and doughnut.
9:47	Joins group of friends discussing forthcoming exams.
9:54	Makes comment while leaving for 10:00 math class: "There just aren't enough hours in the day to get all this studying done."
9:59	Arrives at math class, hopes instructor won't give a quiz over homework assignment.

This student actually studied for less than one-third of a possible sixty-minute study period. The remaining time was squandered in a disorganized attempt to start studying. Unfortunately, disorganization and procrastination are typical of many college freshmen. How about you? How much time did you waste today?

Figure 3.1

Can students afford to waste their time in such aimless activity? Let's look at the study requirements for Terry Gibson, a college freshman whose course load of five academic subjects plus physical education is shown below.

English	3 class hours
Mathematics	3 class hours
Chemistry	3 class hours plus 3 hours of laboratory
History	3 class hours
Spanish	3 class hours
Physical Education	3 class hours

The total time that Terry spends in class and laboratory is only 21 hours per week. However, this schedule does not include the time required for preparation of outside study assignments. The traditional rule of thumb is that the average student needs to spend up to two hours on outside study for every hour spent in class. Let's revise Terry's schedule to include these additional hours of outside study.

"My schedule would be a lot better if my instructors didn't assign so much work."

English	3 class hours and 6 study hours
Mathematics	3 class hours and 6 study hours
Chemistry	3 class hours and 6 study hours plus 3 hours laboratory
History	3 class hours and 6 study hours
Spanish	3 class hours and 6 study hours
Physical Education	3 class hours and 0 study hours

Thirty hours of outside study have been added to the 21 hours spent in the classroom. Now the total time adds up to 51 hours instead of 21. As you can see, being a college student is a time-consuming job.

Fifty-one hours of classes, labs, and study may sound like an impossible requirement at first. However, remember that the 51 hours are spread over seven full days—168 hours. Add 56 hours for sleep to the 51 hours for classes and studying, and you still have 61 hours left for dressing, meals, and recreational activities. Thus, you have plenty of time to carry a full course load, do all your out-of-class studying, work up to 20 hours each week, get sufficient rest, take care of your personal responsibilities, and enjoy a healthy social life—if you manage your time wisely. The important thing is that you learn to manage *all* your time wisely. Efficient time budgeting is absolutely essential for survival in college.

Analyzing Your Uses of Time

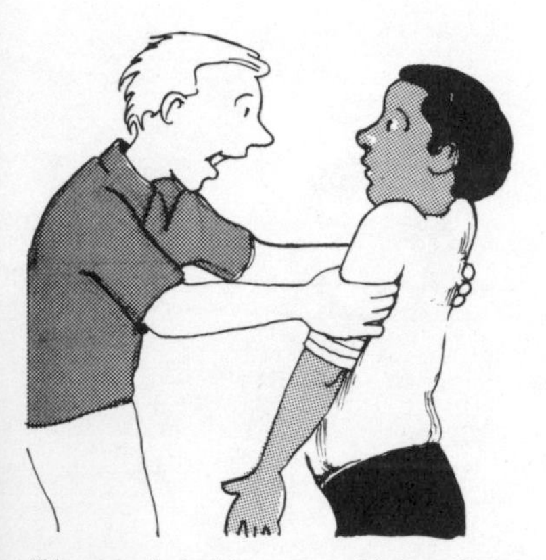

"Hey, am I glad to see you! I thought for a minute that I wouldn't have any excuse not to study!"

A little experiment that you might try can quickly and systematically identify any weaknesses in your present study schedule. Keep a time diary for a period of one week. At the end of each hour during the day make a note of how you spent your time. Don't give yourself credit for studying unless you were actually studying, not daydreaming. At the end of each day count up the number of hours that you really spent studying. You'll probably be surprised to see how much less real studying you do than you think. Look for periods of mixed activity such as studying while listening to the radio. These are usually unproductive and should be eliminated if possible.

If you are at all typical of the majority of students, you may have one or more of the following study problems. First, you don't get as much studying done as you should. Not that you don't try, but somehow you don't manage to accomplish as much as you need to. Second, you waste time going from one thing to another. You try to study too many things during the same day or evening or even during a single hour. Hence, you are so disorganized that you do not stay with one thing long enough to get much done. Finally, you have difficulty settling down to work. You are always getting ready to study, but for one reason or another, a lot of time goes by before you actually start your assignments.

All three difficulties are slightly different aspects of the same problem. When you study, you fail to use your time wisely and to concentrate effectively so that you really accomplish something. Fortunately, these study faults may be corrected. Setting up a schedule for studying is of value to good as well as poor students. A well-planned schedule permits more effective use of time. It keeps you from vacillating about what you are going to do next so that you aren't as disorganized about your studying. It assigns time where time is needed, prevents your studying a subject more than is required, and generally ensures that you are doing the right thing at the right time. With your time thus organized, you will have more time to devote to your most difficult subjects and also more time for activities other than study. A well-planned study schedule minimizes the wasting of prime study time by scheduling study activities to fit individual needs. Also, a properly managed study schedule helps ensure that you have the required materials for study on hand when they are needed.

Time Budgeting Tips

Several general tips may prove helpful to you in distributing your study time.

When preparing for a *participation course* where you will be called upon in class, reserve some time *just before* the class period to study your daily assignment. In this way you will be fresh and ready to do your best work in class.

For a *lecture course,* keep the time *immediately following* the class period free to spend reviewing what was said in class, organizing and expanding your notes so they will be coherent later when you study the reading assignment accompanying the lecture. If, instead, you wait till that night or the next day, you might have difficulty remembering what the instructor had to say. Besides, if the instructor is at all stimulating, you'll be in the best frame of mind to study that topic immediately after the lecture.

Break long periods of study with short relaxation periods. A good rule is to take a five- to ten-minute break after each hour of concentrated study.

Studying a given subject in fairly short, daily periods is far superior to occasional long periods, especially if you need to remember the material later. For example, when you are trying to learn a lot of detailed material, it is much better to study a subject one hour each day for four days than to attempt four hours of study in one day.

Most students who have spent the morning and early afternoon in class or in the library studying find the late afternoon best for recreation and relaxation. Then they are able to resume their studying with renewed vigor for several hours after dinner. It is of great importance that you achieve the proper balance between sleeping, eating, studying, working, and recreation. Experiment until you find the proper balance for you, and then stick to it. *Building habits of regularity is essential to scholastic success.* It requires much practice and self-discipline, but pays dividends in terms of better grades now and better work habits for the future. Remember, the work habits that you develop now will surely influence your future success in your chosen career.

How to Prepare a Time Budget

Efficient time budgeting requires painstaking, systematic planning. The resulting time schedule must be both realistic and practical; that is, it must be sufficiently flexible to handle changing requirements and be adequately balanced between academic work and recreation. For best results, follow this five-step sequence in preparing your schedule.

1. Record Fixed Time Commitments. Write all your regularly scheduled activities such as classes, labs, religious services, employment, band practice, etc. on your schedule.

2. Schedule Daily Living Activities. Set aside ample (but not excessive) time for eating, sleeping, dressing, etc.

3. Schedule Review Time. Reserve time for reviewing either before or after each class, as appropriate. For a lecture course (history, English, etc.), the time immediately following the class period should be kept free for revising and expanding your notes; for a participation course (speech, foreign language, etc.), the time just prior to class should be reserved for reviewing the day's assignment.

4. Schedule Recreation Time. Set aside regular time for such recreational activities as dating, exercising, personal reading, watching television, etc.

5. Schedule Preparation Periods. For each course, schedule sufficient time for preparing outside assignments. The amount of time to be scheduled for each course will depend upon the difficulty level of the material, your ability to master the material, the grade you wish to receive, and the efficiency of your study methods. Preparation periods should be scheduled at times when interference is at a minimum and should be long enough to permit the accomplishment of a significant amount of work. Be sure to write the name of each course in all time periods on your schedule when you plan to study it. Don't just write down "Study."

"For efficient time management, I'd prefer to schedule my history class right after my Spanish class."

Weekly Activity Schedule

Name Terry Gibson　　Date Sept 8

TIME	Monday	Tuesday	Wednesday	Thursday	Friday	Saturday	Sunday	TIME
6:00 6:30								6:00 6:30
7:00 7:30	Breakfast	Breakfast	Breakfast	Breakfast	Breakfast	Breakfast		7:00 7:30
8:00 8:30	History	Study English	History	Study English	History	Work	Breakfast	8:00 8:30
9:00 9:30	Review Hist Review Math		Review Hist Review Math		Review Hist Review Math		Recreation	9:00 9:30
10:00 10:30	Math	English	Math	English	Math	Library Reading	Church	10:00 10:30
11:00 11:30	Study Math	Lunch	Study Math	Lunch	Study Math			11:00 11:30
12:00 12:30	Lunch	Rev Spanish	Lunch	Review Spanish	Lunch	Lunch	Lunch	12:00 12:30
1:00 1:30	Chemistry	Spanish	Chemistry	Spanish	Chemistry	Recreation	Recreation	1:00 1:30
2:00 2:30	P.E	Chem Lab	P.E.	Chem Lab	P.E.			2:00 2:30
3:00 3:30	Recreation		Recreation		Recreation			3:00 3:30
4:00 4:30	Work	Work	Work	Work	Work			4:00 4:30
5:00 5:30								5:00 5:30
6:00 6:30	Dinner	Dinner	Dinner	Dinner	Dinner	Dinner	Dinner	6:00 6:30
7:00 7:30	Recreation	Rec.	Rec.	Rec.	Rec.	Date	Catch-up studying	7:00 7:30
8:00 8:30	Study chem	Study English	Study chem	Study English	Study chem			8:00 8:30
9:00 9:30	Study History	Study Spanish	Study History	Study Spanish	Study History			9:00 9:30
10:00 10:30								10:00 10:30

Figure 3.2

Figure 3.2 is an example of good time budgeting. The student is carrying five academic courses plus physical education, is employed 15 hours per week, and has scheduled 30 hours of outside studying. Note that all entries are clear and specific, that the times set aside for study are realistic and adequate, and that ample time is provided for rest and recreation.

Ten Hints on Time Planning

The following ten suggestions can help you plan your time efficiently. Read the suggestions, then make a study schedule for yourself using the ideas presented. For this purpose, two blank schedule forms are provided at the end of this chapter. You may wish to remove the schedule forms from this book and/or make photocopied enlargements of them on standard-size 8½" x 11" paper. Use one form to prepare a preliminary activity schedule. Live with this tentative schedule for a few days and note whether or not your allotment of study time is really adequate to meet the needs of each of your courses. Also, ask your adviser or a friend to look over your schedule and suggest improvements. Then, prepare a revised schedule in accordance with these suggestions and any new ideas that you might have. Finally, post your final schedule in your room or insert it in the notebook that you carry with you.

1. Schedule Around Fixed Commitments. Some activities have fixed time requirements and others are flexible. The activities that you must consider probably include:

FIXED—classes, religious services, employment, rehearsals, meetings, meals.

FLEXIBLE—sleeping, personal hygiene, dressing, study, recreation.

2. Plan Sufficient Study Time. Most college classes are planned to require up to two hours of outside work per week per credit hour. By multiplying your credit load by two you can get a good idea of the time you may need to provide for studying. Of course, if you are a slow reader, or have other study deficiencies, you may need to plan more time in order to meet the demands of your courses.

3. Set Realistic Study Requirements. You should know from experience about how long it will take you to write a 1500-word English composition, to work 30 algebra problems, to read a 45-page history textbook chapter, or to translate two pages of Spanish sentences. Be realistic in scheduling your preparation time. Don't underestimate!

4. Study at Regular Times and Places. Establishing habits of regularity in studying is extremely important. Knowing what you are going to study, and when, saves a lot of time in making decisions, finding necessary study materials, etc. Avoid generalizations in your schedule such as "study." Commit yourself more definitely to "study history" or "study chemistry" at certain hours.

5. Study as Soon After Class as Possible. Check over lecture notes while they are still fresh in your mind. Start assignments while your memory of the assignment is still accurate. Remember, one hour of study immediately after class is probably better than two hours of study a few days later.

6. Use Free Time for Studying. Those scattered one or two hours of "free" time between classes are easily wasted. Using them for reviewing materials already known from previous study will result in more time for recreational activities later on.

7. Set a Two-Hour Limit. After studying one subject for two hours, many people begin to tire and their ability to concentrate decreases rapidly. To keep up your efficiency, switch to studying another subject after two hours.

"Okay, so I've worked out my study schedule. Now, who's going to make me follow it?"

8. Study Your Hardest Subject First. Begin a long study session by starting with the subject that is the least stimulating or most difficult for you. Not only will your mind be fresh while you are doing your hardest work, but you can switch to something more interesting when you begin to feel fatigued.

9. Study on the Weekends. Some time should always be set aside on the weekends since this is a particularly good time to work on special projects (especially those requiring use of library materials). It is also a good idea to schedule a study session for Sunday evening in order to catch up on back reading or other delayed assignments.

10. Borrow Time—Don't Steal It. Whenever unexpected demands arise that take up time you had planned for study, decide immediately where you can trade for time to make up the missed studying and adjust your schedule for that week accordingly.

Your Study Environment

Successful college students agree that studying is not a social activity. You must learn to isolate yourself from the rest of the world and study alone. There is no other way, for you must create an atmosphere that will permit you to concentrate. A quiet place with proper lighting, ventilation, and the necessary study tools is essential to effective studying. Furthermore, you must learn to discipline yourself so that you can ignore the countless distractions that can destroy your concentration. The ability to concentrate varies greatly from person to person. Some students apparently have little or no trouble concentrating and can study practically anywhere, oblivious to what goes on around them. Others are highly distractible and cannot concentrate unless their study environment is free of distraction. Susceptibility to distraction has been found to be a major problem for most college freshmen.

Where to Study

Students generally study either in the college library or in their own rooms. The conditions under which you study are most important. The result of poor study conditions is twofold. First, concentration is more difficult, with a consequent decrease in understanding and remembering. Second, study time is wasted, with a consequent reduction in time available for recreation and other activities.

Research has consistently demonstrated that the best place to study is the library. This seems quite sensible when you consider that the library is designed specifically for scholarly study. There are fewer distractions—less temptation to put your studying aside—in the library than anywhere else. Also, the reference materials needed for outside assignments are often available only in the library.

Some students are so readily distracted, however, that they have trouble concentrating even in the library. If you find yourself constantly looking around the library for someone you know or would like to know, choose a seat facing a wall in the corner of the room.

Regardless of where you study, your study efficiency is influenced by three environmental factors:

1. Auditory distractions
2. Visual distractions
3. Disorganization

Fortunately, you can evaluate and correct poor study conditions stemming from all three sources. Avoiding distraction requires determined and systematic planning, but pays rewarding dividends in terms of increased study efficiency.

Auditory Distractions

Auditory distractions stem from three major sources:

1. Conversation
2. Electronic media
3. Outside noise

Each type of distraction tends to reduce study efficiency by impairing the ability to concentrate.

Conversation. If you are like most students, you enjoy talking with others about anything and everything. Interacting with others can be both pleasant and valuable, but it should not be allowed to distract you from your studies. Try to avoid all conversation during time set aside for studying. This is especially important at the library, where your conversation will distract other students sitting nearby.

When studying in your room, keep your door closed and perhaps even hang an appropriate sign on the outside. If you have a roommate, either arrange to study at different times or agree to observe "quiet hours" for studying. If both these methods fail, find another place to study. Telephone calls should be discouraged during study time, and unavoidable telephone conversations should be kept as brief as possible.

Electronic Media. Although many students defend the practice, most authorities recommend against studying with a stereo, radio, or television turned on. There are, of course, individuals who study with the stereo, radio, or television on and still make excellent grades. Nevertheless, these media are intended mainly for relaxation and enjoyment. Because they are enjoyable and relaxing, they provide considerable distraction from studying.

Television is the most distracting of the three because two senses—vision and hearing—are stimulated simultaneously. How about a softly playing radio tuned to a program of good music? Even if you aren't distracted by the music itself, the commercials are sure to do the trick.

Of the three media, only the stereo, or other personal sound system, provides the student with a full measure of control over program content. A musical background for studying does appear to help students who find silence and isolation oppressive or use music to filter out more distracting sounds. Your decision about whether to play music when you're studying should depend on the effects on your study efficiency.

Outside Noise. An exciting football broadcast from a neighboring room, shouts accompanying a nearby volleyball game, or traffic sounds from the street are outside noises over which you have little or no control. Noises such as loud talking or singing are more meaningful, and hence more distracting, than are such background noises as passing trains, trucks, and airplanes.

Even though you may be able to concentrate despite such noises, doing so requires added energy so that you become tired of studying more quickly. If you are easily distracted by outside noise, find a quieter spot or change your study time to a quieter time of day!

Visual Distractions

Both the surface of your desk and the space immediately surrounding your study area should be kept free of visual distractions such as photographs, posters, magazines, sports equipment, etc. Glancing at such items may lead you into daydreaming.

An equally distracting situation is produced by placing your desk so that it faces a window or door. Such an arrangement may afford you an excellent view of campus or hallway, but it is unlikely to help you keep your mind on your studies. If you have a roommate, be certain that your desks do not face each other. Such an arrangement is likely to produce more conversation than study.

Disorganization

The third enemy of concentration is lack of organization. One symptom of disorganization is frequently interrupting your studies to sharpen pencils, borrow paper, hunt for missing notes, etc. Eyestrain, sleepiness, and physical discomfort while studying may also indicate poor organization of your study environment.

Working Area. A suitable chair and adequate working space are essential to effective study. The experts advise that you sit in a straight-backed comfortable chair while studying. A chair that is too comfortable will produce sleepiness; one that is too uncomfortable will cause restlessness. Reduced concentration is the result in either case. Also, avoid studying in bed or stretched out on a couch. Both positions are normally associated with relaxation, not with the mild tension required for concentration.

"For some reason, this textbook sure is giving me a headache!"

Your desk should provide ample space for spreading out your materials. Most students find that they need a surface area of at least two feet by three feet. Before you begin studying, clear your desk of everything for which you have no immediate need. Except for your dictionary, notebook, pencils or pens, and erasers, keep only the textbook that you are studying on top of your desk.

Lighting, both natural and artificial, should be evenly distributed over the desk surface, and should not glare on your book or reflect too strongly into your eyes. Indirect lighting is better than direct. High-intensity desk lamps are very useful, but, when trained directly on your reading area, can produce glare and cause eyestrain, headache, and fatigue. Keep these lamps well to the side of what you're studying.

Room temperature and ventilation are also important. Although the ideal conditions are largely a matter of individual preference, studying in a room that is too hot or too cold can cause sleepiness and physical discomfort, while poor ventilation can produce mental sluggishness.

Study Tools. Is your studying often interrupted because the reference books or study materials you need are not on hand? If so, these interruptions can be avoided by systematic planning.

The first step is to prepare a list of needed equipment, reference books, and study materials. The next step is to purchase the needed items and place them within easy reach of your desk. You might use a desk drawer for such items as paper, pencils, erasers, etc. A small bookcase might be desirable for your textbooks, dictionary, thesaurus, etc. The final step is to return items to their proper place after use, and to replenish depleted materials promptly. Remember, effective study organization requires systematic planning, but saves valuable study time.

"Hey, Sam, could you lend me your psych notes? I seem to have lost mine."

Weekly Activity Schedule

Name ______________________________ Date ____________________

TIME	Monday	Tuesday	Wednesday	Thursday	Friday	Saturday	Sunday	TIME
6:00 6:30								6:00 6:30
7:00 7:30								7:00 7:30
8:00 8:30								8:00 8:30
9:00 9:30								9:00 9:30
10:00 10:30								10:00 10:30
11:00 11:30								11:00 11:30
12:00 12:30								12:00 12:30
1:00 1:30								1:00 1:30
2:00 2:30								2:00 2:30
3:00 3:30								3:00 3:30
4:00 4:30								4:00 4:30
5:00 5:30								5:00 5:30
6:00 6:30								6:00 6:30
7:00 7:30								7:00 7:30
8:00 8:30								8:00 8:30
9:00 9:30								9:00 9:30
10:00 10:30								10:00 10:30

Weekly Activity Schedule

Name ______________________ Date ______________

TIME	Monday	Tuesday	Wednesday	Thursday	Friday	Saturday	Sunday	TIME
6:00 6:30								6:00 6:30
7:00 7:30								7:00 7:30
8:00 8:30								8:00 8:30
9:00 9:30								9:00 9:30
10:00 10:30								10:00 10:30
11:00 11:30								11:00 11:30
12:00 12:30								12:00 12:30
1:00 1:30								1:00 1:30
2:00 2:30								2:00 2:30
3:00 3:30								3:00 3:30
4:00 4:30								4:00 4:30
5:00 5:30								5:00 5:30
6:00 6:30								6:00 6:30
7:00 7:30								7:00 7:30
8:00 8:30								8:00 8:30
9:00 9:30								9:00 9:30
10:00 10:30								10:00 10:30

Techniques for Effective Study

Many freshmen find the reading for their college courses to be among their most difficult assignments to handle. Both the amount of assigned reading and the complexity of the material greatly exceed anything that they have previously experienced. If you, like many other freshmen, find your textbooks to be difficult reading, remember that the author of a textbook is trying to provide you with a body of important concepts and facts in a disciplined, scholarly manner. Your part of the bargain is to provide the interest and motivation necessary to master the material.

Another important difference between college and high school textbook reading is that, in college, you will own books and can mark in them all you want to. However, a word of warning is in order. Textbook marking can be a useful aid to study and review, but it must be done with thought and care. Otherwise it can become mere busywork and may give you a false sense of accomplishment when, in fact, you are not really mastering what you are reading at all. Then, too, if you overdo underlining or highlighting, you defeat the purpose of quick identification of important points when you later review the material for an examination.

Professor Francis P. Robinson at Ohio State University devised a simple five-step system for developing higher-level study skills that promotes faster, more meaningful reading, makes it easier to prepare for tests, and can result in appreciably higher course grades. The system is called the *SQ3R Reading Method.* Although this technique will require a little more time while you are reading an assignment, it will greatly reduce the time required for your reviewing before examinations, and you will get much more out of your reviewing. The five steps of the SQ3R Reading Method—Survey, Question, Read, Recite, and Review—are described in detail below.

"That SQ3R stuff only slows you down. I believe in doing my reading fast, so I'll have time for important things."

Using the SQ3R Reading Method will help you in four ways:

1. Organizing material into a meaningful pattern of main ideas and supporting details
2. Increasing your ability to concentrate on what you are studying
3. Learning the information that you will be responsible for in your courses

4. Combatting the tendency to forget what you have learned

The SQ3R Reading Method will work best for you if you also develop the habit of *timely reading.* Timely reading means that you read your textbook assignments at the best possible time—before you go to class to hear the professor's lectures covering the material. This will ensure both better understanding of what the professor says and better class notes. The best time for your first review, of course, is as soon as possible after your professor's lecture on the material.

The SQ3R Reading Method

Step 1: "S" for *Survey.* First, *survey* the reading assignment quickly, taking no more than five minutes to glance over a chapter. Check the headings and subheadings—they represent the author's outline and make it easy for you to follow the organization of ideas. Scan all graphs, maps, tables, diagrams, and pictures—they summarize graphically many facts and relationships that require hundreds of words of text. Read the introductory and summary paragraphs—they point out the main ideas to look for as you read, as well as the relationships of these ideas. Surveying will orient you to what the chapter is all about *before* you study it in detail.

Step 2: "Q" for *Question.* Second, arouse your curiosity about the material by asking yourself the following *question:* "What are the main ideas that the author is trying to tell me about?" Then, as you read, convert headings and subheadings into who, what, where, when, why, and how questions and read to find the answers to these questions. Challenging yourself to find answers to such questions will help to maintain interest in what you are reading and will aid you in evaluating the significance of what you are reading.

Step 3: "R" for *Read.* Third, *read* the assignment carefully for meaning. When you read, do not read passively as you would a novel. Read actively! Underline or highlight key words and phrases to aid you in recalling the main points of the chapter. Use an asterisk, exclamation point, or question mark to indicate an important definition, a significant formula, or a potential test question. Summarize key ideas in your own words in the page margins of the book. Active participation in the reading process will increase your understanding of the material being read.

Step 4: "R" for *Recite.* Fourth, stop at appropriate intervals and *recite* to yourself from memory the main ideas of the assignment, recalling only the points essential to understanding what the author is trying to say. Without looking at the book, check whether you have learned the major concepts by trying to restate them *in your own words.* If you cannot do this immediately after reading the material, you cannot hope to do it tomorrow in class or next week on an exam. Self-recitation provides the best way to test yourself quickly and easily to find out what you have learned. If you can't repeat most of the main points, then you haven't learned the material and you will have to reread it if you are to master what you are studying.

"She's been reciting to herself for over an hour. Should we call Student Health?"

Step 5: "R" for *Review.* Finally, *review* the chapter at periodic intervals to refresh your memory and make the facts stick. Don't wait until you are confronted with an examination to do your reviewing. That's a good time for the final review, but not for the first review. Reviewing is simply the process of going over the material again in order to fix it in your memory. Reread your underlining and marginal notes and restate the sequence of main ideas and supporting facts until you have them once more firmly in mind. Research has demonstrated that the best time to review material is shortly after you have learned it. It is most important, therefore, that you not omit this first review soon after learning. You will, of course, also want to review the material again just before a test.

Taking Lecture Notes

Most students will encounter extensive lecturing for the first time when they enter college. Consequently, very few beginning freshmen know how to take good lecture notes. Yet it is a skill that they must learn very rapidly, for effective note taking, like effective textbook reading, is a must for survival in college.

Students who take few lecture notes, or none at all, sometimes rationalize that note taking distracts them from listening to the lecture, that the professor is too disorganized to follow, or that the lecture only repeats what is in the textbook. The truth of the matter is that there are two very important reasons for taking good lecture notes—to aid you in understanding your professor's presentation, and to aid

"I can't see wasting energy on taking lecture notes. It's all in the textbook anyway."

you in studying for your course examinations. A good lecturer will expand on materials in the textbook by giving fuller explanations and adding more details, and will supplement the textbook by introducing related materials and offering different interpretations.

Good note taking requires you to listen effectively. Effective listening is not easy, for it involves both active *concentration* on what is being said and continuous *evaluation* of what is being said. You should almost always take notes during class. Do not, however, try to write down everything that your professor says. Listen for *meanings* and record only the essentials needed to reconstruct the lecture. Write down the ideas and facts that form the step-by-step development of each topic and then, as soon as possible after class, systematically review, clarify, and expand your notes.

Effective note taking is a skill that will help you both in college and in your future career. Your note-taking skills should improve rapidly if you follow the tips below.

Tips for Improving Your Listening Comprehension

1. Be Prepared. Before going to class, read your textbook assignment and review your notes from the previous class meeting to prepare yourself to get the most out of the lecture.

2. Concentrate on the Lecture. Don't allow yourself to be distracted by your professor's mannerisms, voice quality, or delivery technique. Concentrate on the material, not the way it's conveyed.

3. Listen With an Open Mind. Maintain a questioning, but open-minded, attitude as you listen. You need not accept everything that is said, but don't let your views cause you to reject a new idea before it is fully developed. Write down your questions and points of disagreement so you won't forget them—and continue to listen to the lecture.

4. Keep Physically Alert. Assume a comfortably alert posture in class. Minimize visual or hearing difficulties by sitting up front instead of at the back of the classroom where it is more difficult to pay close attention.

5. Keep Mentally Alert. Avoid doodling in class. Concentrate on the lecture, not on the windows, your watch, or the person sitting next to you. Keep attentive in class by predicting likely test questions, comparing lecture and textbook content, entering into class discussion, etc.

6. Use the Listen-Think-Write Process. Your professors will be speaking at about 100 words per minute, while you can be thinking at about 400 words per minute—a differential ratio of 1:4! Use this extra time for thinking about what is being said. Train yourself to listen attentively to the material being presented, to evaluate critically its importance and the evidence to support it. Then select what is appropriate for your notes and record this in your own words.

Tips for Improving Your Recording Skills

1. Use Outlines. Whenever possible, take your notes in outline form, using a system of enumeration and indentation to distinguish major and minor points.

2. Be Neat. Write legibly and on only one side of the page. This will help you when you review and expand your notes later.

3. Be Orderly. Date and identify each set of notes and keep the notes from different courses separated.

4. Note Study Aids. Copy diagrams, drawings, and other illustrations that your professor puts on the chalkboard.

5. Note Examples. When appropriate, record your professor's examples since they often clarify otherwise abstract ideas.

6. Note Specific Data. Make certain that you record correctly all names, dates, places, formulas, equations, rules, etc.

7. Watch for Emphasis. Keep alert to points that your professor emphasizes by means of repetition, writing on chalkboard, extended comment, etc.

8. Listen for Oral Hints. Keep alert for points your professor emphasizes by means of oral hints. Listen for enumerations such as "the following five steps" or "the four major causes" and for summations such as "consequently" or "therefore." If your professor says, "You'll see this later," or "This is important," follow up such clues by putting an asterisk or other appropriate symbol in the page margin beside your notes.

9. Emphasize Notes. Use symbols, such as an asterisk, a star, or underlining, to indicate points that your professor emphasized.

10. Clarify Notes. Draw a circle around reading and other assignments that are mixed in with your lecture notes. Similarly, circle book titles and other references mentioned by your professor.

11. Note Your Ideas. Separate your own thoughts from those of your professor. Writing down your own ideas, examples, and questions is an excellent way to keep alert during a lecture. For obvious reasons, however, you should bracket or otherwise label these as your own.

"Of all the nerve! Dr. Smith asked questions on stuff in the lectures that isn't in our textbook!"

12. Allow Room to Expand. Leave enough blank space to permit clarifying and expanding your notes later on. Ask a fellow student or your professor to help you fill in the gaps if you think you missed one or more important points.

13. Listen Attentively. Don't be a clock watcher. Your professors cannot always pace themselves accurately, and may cover half of the lecture content in the last ten minutes of class. Pay as close attention to the end of the lecture as you did to the beginning.

14. Expand Notes. Review and clarify your notes as soon as possible after class, but do not waste time on recopying them. Use your page margins to fill in abbreviations, add omitted points, correct errors, etc.

Listening and note taking, like any other skills, will improve rapidly with practice. The important thing is to learn as much as you can in class because this will help you to understand better and to complete your outside assignments. Remember, your professor has worked long and hard to select, organize, and clarify the salient points of the course; taking good notes during lectures will probably save you many hours of hard work later on.

Each of us has experienced the frustration of trying unsuccessfully to remember something that we once knew quite well. Students, as well as professors, find themselves plagued by forgetting as a common everyday experience. It is important, then, that the causes and cures for forgetting be examined and understood.

If you were asked what causes forgetting, you would probably reply that it is due to the passage of time—that unused facts, ideas, and skills gradually fade away with disuse. Although psychologists accept the concept of forgetting through disuse, they offer an abundance of research evidence to prove that this is not the whole story. Their studies show that forgetting as the effect of *interference,* forgetting as the consequence of *underlearning,* and forgetting as a form of *repression* are much more important concepts for understanding why forgetting takes place.

"Forget anything you've learned previously about everything. It's all outdated now as a result of recent discoveries."

Interference

Forgetting through the process of *interference* occurs because new learning gets in the way of recalling old learning and because old learning gets in the way of recalling new learning. Activities occurring between the time something is learned and the time it must be recalled will interfere with remembering the learned material, and the greater the degree of similarity between the later activity and the earlier learning, the less the amount recalled. Your ability to recall something you have learned is also influenced by what you have learned previously. Here, the interference effect on future recall will be greatest where "wrong" information acquired previously must be unlearned and replaced with information which is "right."

Underlearning

Forgetting also occurs as a direct consequence of *underlearning.* Your later recall is likely to be faulty if you learn something inadequately in the first place. Effective learning requires active, not passive, studying of materials. You have to question, to recite, to review—in short, you have to work at learning. Most so-called memory lapses experienced by students probably result from failure to really learn the material in the first place. Underlearning is most likely to exist whenever the material to be learned does not have meaningfulness for you or whenever your learning activity occurs under conditions where concentration is difficult.

Selective Repression

"Well, I still have 40 pages to read, but if I hurry I can be ready to go in half an hour."

Forgetting through the process of *selective repression* occurs because we tend to accept what is consistent with our own interests, values, and prejudices and to reject what does not fit our personal expectations and experiences. Thus our approach to a learning situation may be positive or negative—and there is a world of difference between a positive and a negative attitude. The student with a positive attitude tends to read and listen actively; the student with a negative attitude tends to read and listen passively. If you expect a lecture to be boring, you will find little of interest in the professor's presentation; if you anticipate that a reading assignment will be dull, you will approach the task with indifference or even hostility. Pleasant experiences are remembered much better than unpleasant ones, and we tend to repress the latter from consciousness. The likelihood of repression is increased when your beliefs and values are in marked conflict with the concepts and facts presented in the material that you are expected to learn and remember.

Tips for Improving Your Ability to Remember

Although forgetting cannot be eliminated completely, you can take effective steps to lessen it where remembering is important. Here are a few tips that can help you minimize forgetting.

1. Ensure Meaningfulness. Make sure that you understand the material you are studying. Material that is meaningful to you will be better remembered than things that are unclear. Consequently, you should try to fit new facts into a conceptual framework as you learn them and to tie in new concepts with the body of knowledge that you have already acquired. Try to organize the material by grouping facts and ideas meaningfully, always being alert to similarities and differences. You should also make sure you understand the underlying principles involved *before* you learn a series of isolated factual details.

2. Review Immediately. Most forgetting takes place immediately after initial learning; so an effective technique for improving retention is to use immediate review to test your understanding as you study. Reinforcing memory through immediate review involves more than passively looking over lecture notes and textbook underlining. This process requires active recitation, in your own words, of what you have just heard or read.

3. Overlearn Material. By spending more time studying, many students of average learning ability perform better in college than do others of greater ability. The more thoroughly a skill is learned, the more slowly it is forgotten. Consequently, overlearning is an excellent way to improve retention. So, overlearn! That is, keep studying a subject *beyond* the time required for initial perfect recall. However, remember that a point will be reached after which additional amounts of overlearning will yield diminishing returns.

"Would I learn more chemistry in one eight-hour study period, or in 32 fifteen-minute study periods?"

4. Distribute Learning. Study frequently in shorter periods rather than trying to learn everything all at once. Do not cram if you can avoid it. Retention is generally much better after distributed study than after massed study, so it is usually better to divide your studying of a subject into a number of shorter sessions rather than to mass it into one long session. Be sure, however, that your shorter study sessions are long enough for you to get something done.

5. Use Memory Cues. Develop a system for employing key words and symbols to remind you of important details. When reading a textbook, try to find a key word or phrase that symbolizes the main point in each paragraph. By memorizing a few key words and symbols, you should be able to reconstruct all of the major ideas in the chapter. However, be very careful about using *mnemonic devices* that you may invent or inherit—words, sentences, rhymes, and other formulas that associate a complex principle or body of facts with a simple statement that is easy to remember. The time-honored jingle "Thirty days hath September . . . " is a classic example whereby our calendar's irregularities can be more easily and quickly recalled when needed. However, such memory aids have two major faults—they are unrelated to the intrinsic meaning of the material you are studying, and the slightest error in remembering the rhyme or other formula can throw you off completely.

"Uh-oh! I think I've forgotten the memory cue I was using to learn the material."

6. Practice Restating. Keep expressing the material being learned in your own words. Write it out or say it to yourself or to a friend, restating each point in your own words. You will be required to do this on examinations, so you might as well learn how to express important concepts in your own words right from the start. Expressing the main points in your own words will make it much easier for you to remember them later on.

7. Minimize Interference. Plan your study schedule so that you study your subjects in a sequence that minimizes the effects of the interference process. Since interference is strongest when later learning closely resembles and closely follows earlier learning, try to spread out your studying for courses with similar subject matter content. It would be better for you to study history and chemistry after studying French than immediately to begin studying your Spanish assignment.

"I wouldn't skip so many classes if there was anything worth listening to."

8. Recognize Attitudes. Watch out for negative attitudes! Students tend to attach some degree of affect—liking or disliking, agreeing or disagreeing—to the material being studied. Such emotionally-based feelings about the content and its meaning may cause you to ignore or repress some concepts and to distort or exaggerate the importance of others. To compensate for such subtle, subjective, and unconscious editing of your memory, be alert to conflicts between your beliefs, values, and biases and the concepts and facts presented in the material you are studying. You will remember *what* and *as* you want to remember, so try to approach your learning tasks from a positive rather than a negative viewpoint. Remember, dullness is not inherent in a subject; it is our own attitude that makes something boring. So recognize negative attitudes as hindrances to learning and remembering—and adopt a positive approach to studying.

Taking Examinations

Taking mid-term and final examinations can be the downfall of otherwise capable students. Since course grades are assigned largely on the basis of these exams, students sometimes become nervous and do poorly on a big test by forgetting material that they could previously recall without much trouble. Why? Often, the cause is fear—students know that failure is a very real possibility and they feel that they are inadequately prepared for the exam, or they lack confidence in their test-taking skills. The two keys to conquering such fears are to study the subject matter thoroughly and to develop efficient test-taking techniques.

In high school, the typical pattern is for the teacher to give many small tests, each covering perhaps two chapters of the textbook. Once students have been quizzed on a topic, they are rarely, if ever, tested over that material again. Thus, in high school, many students practice the memorization-regurgitation-forgetting cycle of learning. That is, they wait until the test is announced, then proceed quickly to memorize the information, mostly factual, needed to pass the exam. They then disgorge this memorized material onto their test papers and, afterwards, quickly proceed to forget most of it because the test is now behind them. It is not at all unusual for high school teachers to aid and abet this process by providing practice exercises and study questions that are carefully gone over in class before being asked, in slightly revised form, on a test.

"Poor Dave—he stayed up all night studying for that exam."

In college, you may have as many as six final examinations in a week or two. The exams for your college courses will be much tougher and much more comprehensive than anything that you experienced in high school.

Collectively, your finals may cover up to 3,000 pages of textbook reading, 2,000 pages of other outside reading assignments, and 250 clock hours of lectures and lab activities. Each final examination will cover the entire term and take two or three hours to complete.

So that's what you're up against in college. You *can* succeed, though. It's being done all the time by millions of college students all over the world. What you need to do is to master new methods of preparing for and taking exams. You probably cannot get by in college with the same test-taking techniques that you used in high school.

The questions on college examinations are generally of three types—essay, objective, and problem.

Essay Tests

Essay tests may ask you to "list the causes," "compare the outcomes," or "illustrate these terms" in regard to given topics. In answering essay questions, stick to the point and stop writing when you have exhausted your knowledge. When the directions say to elaborate, that doesn't mean to "pad" your answer with irrelevant and repetitive material!

Objective Tests

Objective tests may vary considerably in structure and method of scoring. The more common types of objective questions you'll encounter in college are true-false, multiple-choice, fill-in, and matching.

Problem Tests

Problem tests usually consist of mathematical or scientific problems to be worked by using a formula or applying a rule, often in a step-by-step process. Here, it is most important that you minimize careless mistakes by checking all computations and the placement of all decimal points.

Perhaps your experience with tests has already given you all the confidence and skill you will need for taking college-level examinations. Because many freshmen, though, need both more confidence and more skill in test taking, here are a few tips that can improve performance on college examinations.

Tips for Preparing for Tests

1. Don't Fall Behind. Keep up with your reading assignments so that studying for an exam will involve only a thorough reviewing and tying together of familiar materials. Frantic last-minute cramming of new material usually undermines confidence and results in faulty remembering.

2. Underline or Highlight. To avoid completely rereading textbook assignments later, prepare them for reviewing by underlining or highlighting key words and phrases and writing summary notes in the page margins as you go along.

3. Clarify. Ask your professor or a competent classmate to clarify material that you do not understand. You cannot remember something unless you first understand it!

4. Review. Review the past material learned in each course at least once every two weeks during the semester. Reread class notes, outside reading notes, textbook underlining, etc.

5. Familiarize Yourself. In reviewing, spend most time on the material that is least familiar, but also review briefly the material that is most familiar.

6. Test Yourself. In reviewing, look for likely test questions and make certain that you can give the correct answer to each in your own words.

7. Study Previous Tests. Keep, correct, and review returned quizzes and exams. Find out what you did wrong so that you won't make the same mistakes again. Previous tests are probably the best source of clues as to what kinds of questions your instructor is likely to ask.

8. Ask Questions. When an exam is announced, ask your instructor what material will be covered and what type of test it will be. Find out as much as possible about the scope and scoring of the test and the nature and form of the questions.

"But this can't *be an essay test! I studied for multiple-choice!"*

9. Study Properly. Orient your studying to the type of exam that has been announced. For an objective test, concentrate on memorizing factual details such as names and formulas. For an essay exam, concentrate on understanding general concepts, principles, and theories. Study for problem-solving tests by working examples of each type of problem that might appear on the exam.

10. Review Briefly. On the night before a big test, quietly rethink the materials through a comprehensive final review and then go to bed early so as to be mentally and physically alert when the time comes to take the exam. Your mind and body will not be fully alert if you have spent most of the previous night cramming.

General Tips for Taking Tests

1. Be on Time. Arrive early so as to be organized and ready instead of in a panic. Go into the test alert but calm. As you work, try to do your best without becoming tense and anxious. Instead of worrying, concentrate on what you are required to do on the test.

2. Don't Panic. Regard lapses of memory as perfectly normal, and do not let them throw you into a panic. If you block on answering one question, leave it for a while and return to it later.

"You'll have to excuse Jeff. He's got a major exam this afternoon."

3. Read the Directions. Make certain that you fully understand the directions for a test before attempting to solve any problems or answer any questions. Don't lower your grade by misunderstanding the directions.

4. Plan Your Time. Plan how you will use your time during the exam. Look quickly over the entire test and then divide your time according to the number and type of questions that you find. Pace yourself; otherwise you will find yourself with insufficient time to answer all the questions.

5. Read Thoroughly. Read each test question carefully and completely before marking or writing your answer. Reread if you are confused. If you still have no idea how to answer a given question, go on to the next one, returning later after you have finished the others.

6. Clarify Questions. Ask your professor for help in interpreting a test question that is unclear or ambiguous to you. The professor will probably want to clear up the misunderstanding for everybody if the question really is misleading or confusing.

7. Do Your Own Work. Be very careful not to give any impression of cheating. Do your own work and do not give *any* help to others. College penalties for cheating typically range from an automatic "F" for the test (or the course) to expulsion from school.

8. Don't Rush. Do not be disturbed about other students finishing before you do. Take your time, don't panic, and you will do much better on the test.

9. Check Your Work. Don't try to be the first one to leave. If you have time left over, edit, check, and proofread your answers. Use all the time available to eliminate careless errors and to make such improvements as you can.

Tips for Taking Essay Tests

1. Read All Questions. Read all the questions through rapidly, jotting down beside each question any pertinent facts or ideas that occur to you. This will give you a good overview of the entire test and help ensure that your answers do not overlap each other.

2. Plan Your Time. Estimate the time that you have for each question according to their relative difficulty and importance. Then keep track of time so that you don't get carried away answering any one question.

3. Answer the Easiest Questions First. Answer the easiest questions first and concentrate on answering one question at a time. Getting down to work on something you can handle is the surest way to reduce your anxiety about tests.

4. Make an Outline. To ensure good organization and prevent careless omissions, make a brief, logical outline for your answer before you start writing. Remember, it's not how much you say, but what you say and how well you say it that counts.

5. Understand the Questions. Decide what kind of answer each question requires before you begin writing. A different kind of answer is required by such action verbs as "illustrate," "list," "define," "trace," "compare," "identify," or "explain."

6. Get to the Point. Avoid long-winded introductions. Your aim in answering most essay questions is to provide the largest amount of point-earning information in the time allowed. A long, irrelevant introduction won't help your score and only wastes your time. Start developing the topic in your first paragraph.

"It's a shame you didn't study—but, if you write well, maybe you'll get some points for saying nothing brilliantly."

7. Include Facts. When appropriate, include factual details to support your answers. Facts demonstrate to your professor that you know what you are talking about.

8. Be Neat. Take time to write legibly and make your corrections, if any, as neat as possible. Most professors react favorably to neatness, so let this work for you. Besides, if your writing is unreadable, few professors will waste their time trying to decipher your answer.

9. Allow Room to Expand. Leave space between your answers. You may need it for new ideas or additional details that occur later when you return to reread what you have written.

10. Do Hard Questions Last. If you encounter a question that you think you can't answer, leave it until last, but don't leave it unanswered. Unanswered questions contribute no points to your score and you may get partial credit for even a poor answer—especially if everyone else has also had trouble with the same question.

11. Check Your Work. Leave enough time to check all your answers for completeness and accuracy of content. Also make sure that there aren't any careless omissions or mistakes in grammar, spelling, and punctuation. You could raise your score simply by correcting an error or adding another fact.

Tips for Taking Objective Tests

1. Do All Questions. Answer *all* questions in order without skipping around. Identify doubtful answers with marks in the margin and check these if time permits after all questions have been answered.

2. Time Yourself. Do not linger too long on any one question. Make your best guess and return later if you have enough time.

3. Watch Wording. On true-false questions, keep alert for negative wording such as "not" or "least," especially when these are not clearly set off through the use of underlining, quotation marks, or capital letters. Watch out also for the use of double or even triple negatives within a sentence. These you must read carefully for understanding instead of merely trying to get by through the cancelling-out process.

4. Watch for Qualifiers. On true-false questions, be alert for qualifying words such as "all-most-some-none," "always-usually-seldom-never," "best-worst," "highest-lowest," or "smallest-largest." When you encounter one of these qualifiers, the best test for truth is to substitute the other members of the series. If your substitution makes a better statement, the question is false; if your substitution does not make a better statement the question is true.

5. Watch for Modifiers. On true-false questions, be alert for modifying or limiting phrases inserted in the statement. Professors sometimes use inserted names, dates, places, and other details to make a statement inaccurate.

6. Watch for Multiple Concepts. On true-false questions, be alert for multiple ideas or concepts within the same statement. All parts of a statement must be true or the entire statement is false.

7. Use the Same Approach. Apply the same approach to answering both true-false and multiple-choice questions.

The same techniques will work equally well for both, since multiple-choice questions are basically true-false questions arranged in groups.

8. Watch Grammar. On multiple-choice questions, be alert for grammatical inconsistencies between the question stem and the answer choices. A choice is almost always wrong if it and the stem do not make a grammatically correct sentence.

9. Match Methodically. On matching exercises, work down one column and match the items of that column, one at a time, against all items in the second column, instead of skipping back and forth between columns looking for a proper match. Make a mark through matches about which you are sure; then it will be easier to match those about which you are uncertain.

Tips for Taking Problem Tests

1. Make Notes. Write down hard-to-remember formulas, equations, rules, etc. after the test begins but before you actually begin working on the test problems.

2. Do What You Can. If you are unable to work a problem, go on to the next one and come back later if time permits.

3. Make an Attempt. Even if you think that your answer is wrong, turn in your work. You may get partial credit if you have used the right process.

4. Be Organized. Show all the steps in your work and clearly identify or label your answer so that it can be quickly found.

5. Check Your Work. Whenever possible, check all answers in a different way from that employed when you first did the work. For example, add down a column of figures when checking if you added up the column when you first solved the problem.

If you practice these tips, you will soon learn to take college examinations in stride. You will also discover that, although their examinations are difficult, your professors will not ask the impossible of you on an exam.

Writing Themes and Reports

Most college freshmen are soon called upon to demonstrate their competency in finding, organizing, and presenting information on an assigned topic. Students are also expected to be able to organize and present their own ideas on a topic of their own choosing. Thus, in addition to examinations, many of your professors will probably use papers written by their students as a basis for assigning course grades. These papers will range from short themes written in class on the basis of your own personal experiences and beliefs to lengthy research reports based on systematic and comprehensive library study.

Keep in mind that the grading of all papers—themes, essays, critiques, reports, etc.—is a subjective process, and that individual differences exist among professors. Despite these differences, though, your professors will generally be influenced by six factors in deciding your grade on a theme or report. Take these factors into consideration as you plan and prepare any written assignment.

"Oh, by the way, there's one small detail. If I find more than three errors in spelling, punctuation, or grammar, I'll cheerfully give you an 'F' on your paper."

1. *Appearance:* overall attractiveness of your paper as reflected by neatness, legibility, etc.

2. *Organization:* overall coherence of your composition as evidenced by logical and effective presentation of material.

3. *Originality:* self-expression as reflected by the effective presentation of your own ideas and the uniqueness of your approach.

4. *Variety:* comprehensiveness of coverage as indicated by the number and types of reference sources you have used.

5. *Mechanics:* your command of Standard English as reflected by correctness of grammar, syntax, diction, spelling, punctuation, and capitalization.

6. *Format:* your adherence to correct form by proper use of footnotes, bibliography, section headings, margins, etc.

Many freshmen have difficulty with the short, in-class themes commonly required in first-year English courses. If you find in-class themes difficult, the following suggestions should help you to improve your ability at this type of writing assignment.

1. **Keep Calm.** Panic will lower your working efficiency and increase the likelihood of your making errors.

2. **Choose Your Topic Carefully.** When you are given a choice, choose your theme topic with the utmost care. Your topic selection should be based upon your familiarity with and interest in the various possible subjects. Do not decide hastily, for this is your first and most important step.

3. **Be Prepared.** If your theme topic is known beforehand, go into class mentally prepared with a reservoir of factual information about your subject.

4. **Use Your Experience.** If your theme topic is unknown beforehand, draw on your own experiences as much as you can. Avoid experimentation with unfamiliar subjects when you are pressed for time.

5. **Be Specific.** Make your subject suitable for a short theme. Narrow down your topic to a specific, essential, and interesting phase of the broad subject.

6. **Gather Facts.** Allow yourself a few minutes to think about the subject and jot down ideas to be presented. Quickly list both major concepts and important supporting facts as these come to mind.

7. **Outline.** Organize your ideas into a brief, logical outline before you begin writing. Use cue words and phrases instead of complete sentences. Outlining makes for better organization and presentation of your ideas.

8. **Be Concise.** Do not pad! Quality is more important than length in determining the grade you will receive.

9. **Watch Your Vocabulary.** Use words that you understand and can spell. Avoid both stilted language and slang.

10. **Use Short Sentences.** Unless you are good at punctuation, avoid long sentences requiring complex internal punctuation.

11. Use Facts. Be concise and concrete. Give evidence and facts to support your ideas and conclusions whenever possible.

12. Edit as You Write. Check for readability as you write your theme. Pay attention to coherence, to transition, to emphasis, and to smoothness.

13. Be Neat. Write legibly and make all corrections neatly. Neatness indicates pride in your work and makes a good impression before your professor starts reading.

14. Reread. Allow a few minutes to reread and polish your theme, carefully checking for correctness of grammar, punctuation, and spelling.

15. Don't Recopy. Make your first draft your final one. Usually time will be too limited for recopying.

Tips for Writing Research Reports

Writing term papers and other research reports introduces you to the basic procedures essential for scholarly thought and disciplined inquiry. Planning, preparing, and writing a research paper will help you to develop five highly important skills—skills that you will be called upon to use repeatedly in future employment, in family life, and in many other settings.

First, research experience will develop your ability to *locate* comprehensive information on a given topic. Second, it will develop your ability to *understand* the information once you have found it. Third, it will develop your ability to *evaluate* the accuracy and usefulness of the information. Fourth, it will develop your ability to meaningfully and systematically *organize* information drawn from a variety of sources representing several viewpoints. Finally, it will develop your ability to clearly and effectively *communicate* the obtained information to others needing the knowledge.

The research paper has become a standard assignment in many courses at almost all colleges. Writing a research report is a much more ambitious and demanding activity than is the writing of an in-class theme. You will normally go through the following seven steps in writing a research paper:

1. Choosing your topic
2. Locating sources of information

3. Collecting pertinent information
4. Organizing the obtained information
5. Writing your first draft
6. Revising your rough draft
7. Preparing your finished report

Suggestions are given below for each of these seven steps.

SELECTING YOUR TOPIC

1. Understand the Assignment. Listen to your professor's instructions about the purpose, nature, scope, and limits of the assignment. Be certain that you know precisely what kind of paper you are expected to write, how long it should be, and when it is due.

2. Pick a Good Topic. Choose a topic that really interests you—something that is intriguing, exciting, and personal. You will generally have greater confidence and do better work with a topic that has some special meaning for you, that you know something about, or that you have had some experience with.

"I admire Bob's style. He sure knows how to pick a research topic."

3. Make Sure References Are Available. Choose a subject for which you can locate pertinent and up-to-date information. If in doubt, consult the librarian to make sure that your library has all or most of the references that you will need to consult.

4. Vary Your References. Choose a topic that will allow you to use a variety of information sources such as books, special encyclopedias, professional journals, popular magazines, newspapers, personal interviews, or original experiments. Remember, a main purpose of the assignment is to help you become skillful in using the basic tools of scholarship and disciplined inquiry.

5. Be Practical. Choose a topic that is challenging but not too complex to understand in the time available. The subject you select should be one that you can feel comfortable with, given your present level of training and experience.

6. Pick a Worthwhile Topic. Choose a topic that is not too narrow or trivial. The amount of reference material available to you may be inadequate if your topic is too small.

7. Set Some Limits. Choose a topic that is not too broad or ambitious for the assigned length of the paper and the time available to write it. Be certain that you can adjust the focus of your topic to the length and due date of your paper.

8. Be Objective. Choose a topic that is not too controversial for you to handle with objectivity. When you write on an emotionally charged subject, you will very likely find yourself taking sides, presenting mainly your view of the controversy and failing to present other views adequately.

LOCATING SOURCES OF INFORMATION

1. Define Your Purpose. Prepare a brief, precise *thesis statement* defining the objective and scope of your paper. The thesis statement will serve as a point of reference as you seek information on your topic.

2. Compile References. Use the campus library's card catalog or computerized catalog plus appropriate indexes, abstracts, and guides to build up a comprehensive bibliography of pertinent references on your topic.

"Why so many reference books? Read one and you've read 'em all."

3. Select References. Quickly survey each book or article to determine whether or not it contains the kind of information you want. If the material is relevant to your topic, prepare a bibliography card that includes all the information necessary for your future footnotes and bibliography.

4. Check New Sources. Check the references cited in materials that are pertinent to your topic. Bibliography building usually becomes a chain reaction with one source providing clues to additional sources.

5. Obtain Your Own Data. If necessary and feasible, develop and use first-hand information sources such as personal interviews or original experimentation.

6. Note Other Sources. Keep an "idea page" in your notebook for jotting down possible sources of information suggested during lectures and conversations or encountered while reading.

COLLECTING PERTINENT INFORMATION

1. Make Notes. Take brief, accurate, pertinent, usable, readable notes *in your own words.* Avoid the tendency to copy material word for word.

2. Use Index Cards. Take your notes on 3" x 5" or 4" x 6" cards. Use a separate card for each major idea and each reference source. This way, it will be easy to arrange the major ideas in logical order. Be sure to identify the reference source on the back of each card.

3. Keep to the Point. Use your thesis statement as a guide to keep you on the subject while taking notes. Be sure that your notes really pertain to the subject and that you aren't departing from the objective and scope stated for your paper.

ORGANIZING YOUR INFORMATION

1. Organize Your Cards. Read through your note cards and sort them into groups according to whatever categories seem logical to you. All cards dealing with the same subtopic should be placed together.

2. Weed Out Cards. Determine what appears to be the central theme for each group of cards. Scan all cards in the group and eliminate any duplications and irrelevancies that you discover. Then organize each group of cards into the most logical sequence.

3. Organize Major Ideas. Arrange the groups of cards into the most appropriate order to achieve the best possible organization of your major ideas. When you feel that the cards are organized satisfactorily, number each card according to your final order of arrangement.

"Poor Diane. She's been trying for two hours to outline that research paper she wrote last week."

4. Outline Your Paper. Using your organized note cards as a guide, prepare a detailed outline for your paper. Keep this outline simple and direct by using cue words and phrases instead of complete sentences. You can return later to polish up this tentative outline.

WRITING YOUR FIRST DRAFT

1. Think Onto Paper. With your tentative outline before you, start the first draft of your paper. Write in longhand, or on a typewriter, or on a computer or word processor—whatever is most convenient for you. The main point is to get some rough ideas onto paper as spontaneously as possible so you'll have something to build on.

2. Develop Your Topic. Elaborate on your topic wherever supporting ideas and details occur to you. At this point, don't be too concerned about spelling, punctuation, or grammar. Use uncomplicated sentences and familiar words. Concentrate on building up your topic; you can polish the language later.

3. Divide Your Paper. Organize your paper into the following divisions—introduction and description of subject, full discussion of subject, summary and conclusions.

4. Make Your Points. Stick to the thesis of your paper and avoid digressions. For each major idea, get to the point quickly and then systematically and logically develop the thought through examples and explanations.

5. Cite Facts. Include concrete examples, illustrations, and factual details to back up your assertions. Ideas expressed as generalities without supporting facts are neither convincing nor interesting reading.

6. Expand. Do not be reluctant to criticize, evaluate, illustrate, attack, or defend where appropriate to your topic. Show that you have been thinking instead of merely copying.

"I can't remember where I got these quotations. Do you think the prof will catch on if I just make up some references?"

7. Note Reference Placement. As you write, indicate your information sources by placing the number of the note card for a reference in the page margin beside the idea. This will make it easy for you to return later to complete the footnoting of your references after you have prepared your alphabetical bibliography.

8. Allow Space for Revision. Leave plenty of room for later correcting and editing. Wide margins and double-spacing will make it easier to insert the many additions and corrections that will be necessary.

REVISING YOUR ROUGH DRAFT

1. Wait Before Rereading. Set your first draft aside and allow yourself a "cooling off" period. After a couple of days, you'll be able to reread your rough draft with greater objectivity.

2. Improve Your Vocabulary. Use a dictionary or thesaurus to help you find the exact word to express an idea or to find alternative words for those that you might be overusing. Don't use unfamiliar or uncommon words unless you're sure that you're using them correctly.

3. Check Your Style. Check your paper for overall effectiveness of expression. Look at your sentence structure and paragraphing for clarity, smoothness, and effectiveness. Read for logical progression and smooth transition between the main thoughts in your paper.

4. "Tighten" Your Paper. Eliminate excessive or repetitious wording wherever possible. Express your thoughts as briefly and precisely as you can.

5. Proofread. Carefully check your paper for mechanical errors such as misspelled words, inaccurate punctuation, and incorrect grammar.

6. Look for Errors. Profit from your previous mistakes and don't make the same errors again. Carefully check your paper against returned papers for mechanical and stylistic errors that you have made previously.

7. Check Footnotes. Watch carefully to prevent any possibility of plagiarism. Be absolutely certain that your footnoting gives full credit for all materials used directly or in paraphrased form.

"Instead of revising my first draft, I decided it would be easier just to write a new paper."

PREPARING YOUR FINISHED REPORT

1. Type Your Paper. If possible, type the final version of your report. Follow your professor's guidelines carefully. Usually, papers should be double-spaced and have generous page margins. If you use a computer or word processor, be sure that the printer provides crisp, legible copy.

2. Check the Format. Follow the exact format prescribed by your professor for the title page, table of contents, bibliography, footnotes, etc. The prescribed format may vary from course to course, so check with your professor if you are in doubt.

3. Plan Your Time. Avoid the frantic, last-minute rush that can lead to careless errors. Allow yourself plenty of time to complete the paper calmly and correctly.

4. Recheck Your References. Doublecheck your footnoting against your alphabetized bibliography. Make certain that all of your footnotes are accurately tied to the references listed in your bibliography.

5. Proofread Your Final Draft. Be sure to give the final draft of your report one last proofreading for careless errors—misspelling, punctuation errors, omitted words, etc.

"Do you think Dr. Carr will accept my first draft? I just don't have time to copy it over."

6. Present Your Paper. Submit your report on time and follow your professor's instructions about whether it should be stapled, paperclipped, or put in a binder. Let your punctuality and neatness show that you have pride in your effort.

If you follow the preceding steps, your ability to handle term papers and research reports should quickly show improvement. In addition to these suggestions, however, you will also have to follow the technical procedures required for using quotations, footnoting references, and preparing the bibliography. Style guides for dealing with these matters are available in your college library or bookstore. Consult a style guide before you begin working on your first research paper and keep it handy for future reference.

Start to work on your paper immediately upon receiving the assignment. Complete your research and reading well ahead of the deadline for your paper. The earlier you get started, the less difficult your task will be.

"Yes, it is an inspiring sight—except that I told them I want their papers by the 11th."

Motivation for Effective Study

Beginning college freshmen quickly discover that they are expected to assume responsibility and exercise self-discipline over their personal, social, and academic activities. For some, this is a major adjustment. If you are to survive as an entering freshman, you must realize that the first year in college is *not* grade 13 of high school.

Putting Studies First

Surviving your first year of college depends largely on your ability to handle your new freedoms and responsibilities in an adult manner. Adults are expected to exercise self-discipline and attend to first things first. One measure of maturity is the ability and willingness to accomplish the things that *must* be done, even if that sometimes means putting off leisure activities. What about you? Will you be able to put your studies ahead of your social life?

"If Bill and I'd had any sense, we would have waited until after finals to have a fight."

Psychologists point out that many human problems stem from the conflict of short-range needs and interests with long-range goals. Interest in the opposite sex, desire for more spending money, and enjoyment of personal liberty are normal and important concerns of college students. You owe it to yourself, though, not to allow these immediate needs to interfere with such long-range goals as preparing for a future occupation and developing a meaningful philosophy of life.

Keeping in Good Health

Your physical and mental health are important factors influencing your success in college. If you encounter unexpected difficulty in handling your college work, one of the first things to check is your physical health. If you need glasses or are always tired, you won't be able to concentrate on your studies. Likewise, excessive nervousness, frequent headaches, or other physical complaints may also reduce your study efficiency. Consult the student health clinic about any health problems that may be influencing your college work.

Learning to Think Positively

Good mental health includes having a positive outlook on life and thinking positively when you react to a problem. What is your attitude about college—positive or negative? You will have both pleasant and unpleasant experiences during your college years. It is your attitude that will determine how you deal with them. If your attitude is generally positive, you will focus your attention on the more challenging and satisfying aspects of academic activity; if your attitude is negative, you will concentrate on the unpleasant aspects. Think positively and you will see college as a stimulating and exciting experience; think negatively and you will view college as dull and unrewarding.

Obviously, then, having a positive attitude is a key to success in college. A positive attitude keeps you motivated, alert, and productive, whereas negative thinking saps your energy and enthusiasm. Positive thinking lets you relax and enjoy the experience of college life, while a negative attitude causes you to miss out on much of the fun that college offers. Your fellow students and your professors will probably like you more if you display a positive attitude, while a negative attitude will make most people want to keep as far away from you as possible. All in all, you pay a steep price when you let negative attitudes control your mental outlook.

"There goes one guy who could use a big change in attitude!"

What can you do to change your attitude from negative to positive? One answer is to take another look! Look for those things that are good, pleasant, and right instead of those that are bad, unpleasant, and wrong about your situation. When your professors turn on the pressure and assignments start to pile up, you may begin to feel that college isn't worthwhile. But take a second look! What about all the stimulating friendships, the satisfaction of mastering intellectually exciting ideas, the feeling of accomplishment in achieving new skills, as well as the enjoyment of personal freedom, social life, sports, and other extracurricular activities that form a major part of college life? Remember, there are two sides to every problem or situation—so think positively and don't let a negative attitude interfere with your college career.

Achieving Grades

College students often criticize grading practices, especially when their own grades are low. It is wise to remember that your professor does not earn your grades—you do. Even so, professors often blame themselves, at least partly, when a student gets low grades. Inability to help a student perform up to potential is especially frustrating to the dedicated teacher. So, if your grades aren't all that you'd like, be fair enough not to place the blame on your professors. Accept the fact that only you can be responsible for achieving the grades that you want.

Making Academic Decisions

A great many freshmen are uncertain about their future educational and vocational plans. They are vague or unrealistic about the occupational field they plan to enter; consequently, they are undecided as to what their major and minor subjects should be. All too often, the result of such indecision is lack of interest in their studies.

"I could have gotten an 'A' if Dr. Jones had known how to teach the material."

Three of the major symptoms of lack of interest in studies are procrastination, vacillation, and disorganization. *Procrastination* is most often characterized by delay and distraction in completing academic activities. The procrastinator, for example, delays reading assignments until just before an examination, then tries to catch up through frantic, last-minute cramming. *Vacillation* is most often characterized by fluctuating feelings toward academic activities and requirements. The vacillator may be interested today, indifferent tomorrow, bored the next day, then reverse the cycle the following week. *Disorganization* is most often characterized by confusion and disorder in working on academic activities. Forgotten assignments, misplaced books, jumbled notes, and a cluttered desk typify the disorganized student.

If procrastination, vacillation, and disorganization characterize your study behavior, you can benefit by systematically examining your academic goals. Your scholastic motivation is likely to remain low until you clarify your educational objectives. One of the keys to a good academic attitude is knowing what you want from college and why you want it.

It's up to You

The general suggestions offered in this book are intended to encourage you to think positively and take constructive action. The development of efficient study habits and positive academic attitudes may require considerable investment of time and effort. However, you should soon see a significant improvement in your academic achievement if you work at developing more effective study skills by following the suggestions that have been offered.

Many of the better paying and more fulfilling jobs require college training. The college graduate has a much better opportunity to do creative or managerial work than does the high school graduate. Better pay, greater security, higher prestige are but three of the occupational rewards for completing college. You should consider each one long and hard if you sometimes find yourself getting discouraged by the amount of time and effort that your courses require. For many students, the stimulating intellectual environment of the college campus challenges them for the first time to deepen their self-understanding, their awareness of science and technology, their appreciation of human thought and literature through the centuries, and their understanding of cultures elsewhere in the world. In the future, these spiritual, intellectual, and emotional rewards of a college education are likely to prove even more crucial for a life full of rich meaning than they have in the past.

You can succeed at earning these, and other, rewards of a college education. Good luck!

"My only problem is going to be remembering to follow all the suggestions in my Guide to College Survival.*"*